INVOKING THE GLORY

PRAYERS TO INVOKE THE GLORY OF LORD 2021 AND BEYOND

I0155420

Restoration of the Breach
WITHOUT BORDERS

West Palm Beach, Florida

PROPHET REVEREND
KAREL DAWES

ISBN: 978-1-954755-13-0

Published by:
Restoration of the Breach without Borders
133 45th Street, Building A7
West Palm, Florida 33407
restorativeauthor@gmail.com
Tele: (561) 388-2949

EBook Cover Design by:
Tevaugn Brown
tbartgraphics@gmail.com

Editing done by: Claudia Johnson
cjcarr38@gmail.com

Formatting and Publishing done by Sherene
Morrison
Publisher.20@aol.com

Unless otherwise stated Scripture verses are quoted
from the New King James Version of the Bible.

TABLE OF CONTENTS

Dedication   5

Endorsements   6

Acknowledgements   9

Introduction   12

What Is The Glory Of God?   28

Invoking The Glory Of The Lord From
The Canonized Scriptures   48

Praying For The Glory From The
Book Of Exodus   48

Praying For The Glory From
The Book Of Numbers   53

Praying For The Glory From The Book
Of Deuteronomy   54

Praying For The Glory From The Book
Of Judges   55

Praying For The Glory From The Book
Of 1 Kings   56

Praying For The Glory From The
Book Of 1 Chronicles   57

Praying For The Glory From The
Book Of Nehemiah   59

Praying For The Glory From The
Book Of Psalm   60

Praying For The Glory From The
Book Of Isaiah   69

Praying For The Glory From The
Book Of Ezekiel   76

Praying For The Glory From The
Book Of Habakkuk   90

Praying For The Glory From The
Book Of Matthew   93

Praying For The Glory From The
Book Of Mark   95

Praying For The Glory From The
Book Of Luke   96

Praying For The Glory From The
Book Of John   98

Praying For The Glory From The
Book Of Acts   101

Praying For The Glory From The
Book Of Romans   103

Praying For The Glory From The
Book Of Corinthians   104

Praying For The Glory From The
Book Of Ephesians   105

Praying For The Glory From The
Book Of Colossians   106

Praying For The Glory From The
Book Of 1 Thessalonians   107

Praying For The Glory From The
Book Of Hebrews   107

Praying For The Glory From The
Book Of 1 Peter   109

Praying For The Glory From The
Book Of Revelation   111

Invoking The Glory Of The Lord
From The Apocrypha   113

Praying For The Glory From 1 Esdras   113

Praying For The Glory From 2 Esdras   114

Praying For The Glory From Tobit   119

Praying For The Glory From The
Wisdom Of Solomon   120

Praying For The Glory From Sirach   121

Praying For The Glory From Baruch   124

Praying For The Glory From
Additions To The Book Of Esther   128

Praying For The Glory From
Additions To The Book Of Daniel   129

Praying For The Glory From 2 Maccabees   130

About The Author   132

DEDICATION

This book is dedicated to the King of Glory, my Lord and Saviour, the Lord Jesus Christ of Nazareth, without whom none of this would have been possible (John 1:3; Col. 1:15-17). To Him be all glory, yesterday, today and forever!

ENDORSEMENTS

This is an inspiring and scripturally sound book on prayers to invoke the glory of the Lord. For those of us who wants to live an exciting and victorious Christian life, this is an excellent guide.

-Apostle Bishop Devon Laird (PhD).
Diocesan Bishop
New   Bethel
International Ministries.
Canada
* * * * *

Karel is numbered as an end time vessel for our Lord Jesus Christ. She is fearless, full of faith as she becomes more and more courageous with each new revelation from the Lord. She stands as a general amongst the women of faith spanning past, present and future generations. She is one who has shared numerous extraordinary encounters with the Lord Jesus Christ, who has ushered her to move from faith to faith and from glory to glory as she does exploits in uncharted realms for her Master. As she obeyed the Lord to pray for the glory of the Lord, the church witnessed the manifest glory of the Angel of His presence in our midst.

May the Holy Spirit use this book as inspired by the King of Glory, the Lord of Hosts, to open each readers' eyes to see the awesome power of His glory in action through and around ordinary humanity when we live in obedience to Him. The Lord does not share His glory with other gods, rather He uses His glory to transform lives to share in His full weight and heaviness. "And we all, who with unveiled faces contemplate the Lord's glory, are being transformed into his image with ever-increasing glory, which comes from the Lord, who is the Spirit" (2 Cor. 3:18).

Let us as the Body of Christ, earnestly pray for the glory of the Lord.

-Minister Herfa Brown (Mrs.)
Holy Living Christian Ministries and
Senior Probation Officer Jamaica

ACKNOWLEDGEMENTS

For more than a decade I have been hearing: You will write books. However, feelings of intimidation prevented same from happening before now. It wasn't until I saw and heard angels shouting: write...pray for the glory of the Lord; and the Lord subsequently speaking to me saying: Tell them! That I gained the confidence needed to obey Him.

It is for this reason I acknowledge the Holy Spirit, the Helper, Strengthener given us by Christ (John 16:7), whose full weight and heaviness has been poured out upon my life to empower me to obey Christ to compile and deliver the words and prayers written in this book. Thank you Lord for entrusting me with this assignment, necessary to prepare the assemblies of God for the glory needed for the darkness ahead, for when there was darkness in Egypt the GLORY of the Lord was over the children's dwellings (Ex.10:23, Isa. 4:5).

To a wonderful friend and brother, Rev. Leostone Morrison, who by his commitment to bible study teachings, gave himself to hear the heart of God that he may give us MIND RENEWAL. My brother, thank you for your role in paving the way for a friend to overcome her limitations. Rev. Morrison shared the experiences he had gained and the relationships that he had developed to help me become 'a better me'.

Much appreciation to the Editor, Mrs. Johnson-Larmond, the Graphic Designer, Tevaun Brown and the Publisher, Mrs. Sherine Morrison, without your contributions the end product could not have been achieved.

Apostle Bishop Devon T. Laird (PhD) and Pastor Leonie, thank you both for your continuous support, prayers and encouragement. To

Minister Herfa and all the brethren who believed, to those who will believe the word given me and share in His glory, thank you for allowing me into your space.

Very special credit to my children and my extended family members, for understanding the call upon my life and loving me enough to dole me out to the Body of Christ. To My beloved husband, thank you for embracing the changes that you have witnessed occurring as you share me with the Lord Jesus Christ. Bless you for trusting the King of Glory with your wife!

INTRODUCTION

I write this book in total obedience to the Lord Jesus Christ of Nazareth, our Lord and Saviour and soon coming King.

We are in the last days. Between November and December 2020, on the occasions that I sought the Lord in prayer at my altar, I kept hearing myself crying out to the Lord to soak me in His glory. This happened several times. I had never prayed like that before, so the utterings got my attention in a new way. I began to ponder that this was not in my consciousness, because I did not set out to pray for the glory. I quickly deduced that this must be the Holy Spirit who was praying through me.

This sparked an interest in me to begin to research the glory of the Lord. I found some scriptures and I decided to print them and to pray them. That night before going to bed, I sent the scriptures I found to my son. It was exactly 12:02 AM December 30, 2020, asking him to print them for me in the morning. Just before daybreak on December 30, 2020, the Lord gave me one of several visions. In this particular vision, I saw people in the clouds looking down from heaven. They all looked alike and they were very far away in the skies. They were calling out to me from afar. Their voices echoed calling out my name, and my name echoed across the skies, as they shouted and beckoned to me saying: "Karel, pray for the glory of the Lord," I answered them and said to them "Yes, I have found the scriptures and I am going to print them and begin to pray them." Then in one accord, with an echoing voice they shouted to me: "Nooo! you have to write the scriptures down. You have to write them down and pray for the glory of the Lord." I answered them and said, "Ok, I will write them down." But while responding to them, I was thinking what a mammoth task that will be, because it was a lot of Scriptures which spoke of the glory of the Lord. Nevertheless, despite thinking how challenging this would be, I said, "Yes I will." and immediately I heard the voice of the Lord, talking to me.

The Lord said, "There is darkness that is coming upon the face of the earth. Dark days are ahead, but tell my people to pray for My glory. Because when there was darkness in Egypt there was light in Goshen. My glory was that light which shone in, around and over Goshen. He said: "Pray for My glory, pray for My kabod, for in My glory, in My kabod shall no sickness dwell. No virus, no germs, nor diseases, or radiation can penetrate My glory. Pray for My kabod and My kabod will come. Tell the church My people, to pray for My kabod, because I am coming again soon. I am coming for a glorious church. Therefore, My glory must return to the church before My appearance. Pray for My glory, My kabod will come and be your kabod."

Just before coming out of that vision, the Lord said to me, with great power and a stern voice: "It is important for you to pray for My glory. Go and tell them about My "G"! Go tell them about My glory, My glory, My kabod!" I came out of the vison speaking in tongues and worshiping the Lord, as this was how I was responding to him as He spoke with me.

In the days that followed, I began to do that which he commissioned me to do. As I began to write out each of the scripture in my Prayer Journal, He would tell me what to pray and that I was to write it below each scripture to which He led me.

The Lord continued to talk with me throughout the experience. He said "My kabod means liver. I researched the Hebrew word for glory, which is kabod and interestingly one of its meanings is liver. The Lord said: "I am the giver of life, the resurrection and the life, though you be dead, yet shall you live! I cause you to live and not just live for now but live eternally." He showed me that everything in scripture from beginning to end is about the glory of the one true and living God. He said, "Everything in My Holy Scripture speaks of Me. I am the King of Glory."

My research highlighted that the organ known as the Liver, main function is to remove impurities from the blood. The Bible says in Lev. 17:11 & 14 "life is in the blood". The liver also breaks down medication, builds protein in the body and that is what it is made to do. The Lord explained to me that the liver is also called the kabod, which is the glory. My glory, My full weight and heaviness. He then said to me, "My liver, My kabod will come and be your kabod, My liver will come and be your liver to protect you. Tell my people, my church that they do not need this particular vaccine. Tell My people, to pray for My glory and come into My glory for when they begin to pray for My glory, My glory will come and be a shield around them, their glory and the lifter up of their heads. It shall be shield, a force field that nothing can penetrate to harm those who belong to Me."

Just before watch night service, on December 31, 2020, people were contacting me to ask what seed offering they were to sow to enter into 2021. I told them that God did not tell me anything about sowing a seed offering for 2021. Therefore, I cannot tell them about a monetary seed to sow for 2021. I told those who contacted me that if they desired to sow into the Body of Christ, they were to go into their prayer closet and seek the Lord concerning that which they desired to know. I told them that what He has told me, is to tell you to pray for His glory. I told the church as instructed. The Lord said: "Tell them when they begin to pray for My glory, My glory will come upon the church in 2021. Guide the people to pray for My glory. Dark days are coming and only in My glory will you be protected. My glory will come and be a shield around you, a force field that no sicknesses, viruses, diseases or radiation can penetrate. I'm coming soon and I'm coming back for a glorious church, pray for My glory!"

On January 01, 2021 the Lord again spoke to me. He said, "This is why I did not tell you about a seed for 2021: **no amount of seed offering can invoke Me for My glory.** What the church need is My glory. Tell My people to pray for My glory, for only in My kabod will they be safe! All they need to pray for in 2021 and beyond, until I tell them differently is to ask Me for My glory. For only in My glory, My kabod, in My full weight and heaviness, only in My glory will they be able to withstand what is coming."

The Lord led me to more scriptures. He told me to write them and begin to pray them and His glory will come and I will see His glory. We began as a church to pray for the glory each time we gathered. On February 28, 2021, we at Holy Living Christian Ministries began to see the glory of the Lord. Since then, His glory and the Angel of His presence has been manifesting all around us, (Refer to pictures below) in our services, our baptisms and in our homes. Thanks be to God, no one in our congregation or our families, relatives and friends who have heard, believed and obeyed the word of the Lord has become sick. Because the Lord said onto me, "tell them, when they begin to pray for My glory, I, the Lord will create above every dwelling place of Mount Zion, and above her assemblies, a cloud and smoke by day and the shining of a flaming fire by night. For over all the glory there will be a covering," (Isa. 4:5). Hallelujah thanks be to God!

I pray that you will join us and begin to pray for the glory of the Lord. May your lives never be the same as the King of Glory settle His, kabod, His full weight and heaviness upon you in 2021 and beyond.

God bless you!

Fig. 1 February 28, 2021, people reported seeing a light shone all around me as I stepped into the river for baptism. It was caught on camera as it shone all around us as our faces gleamed in His glory.

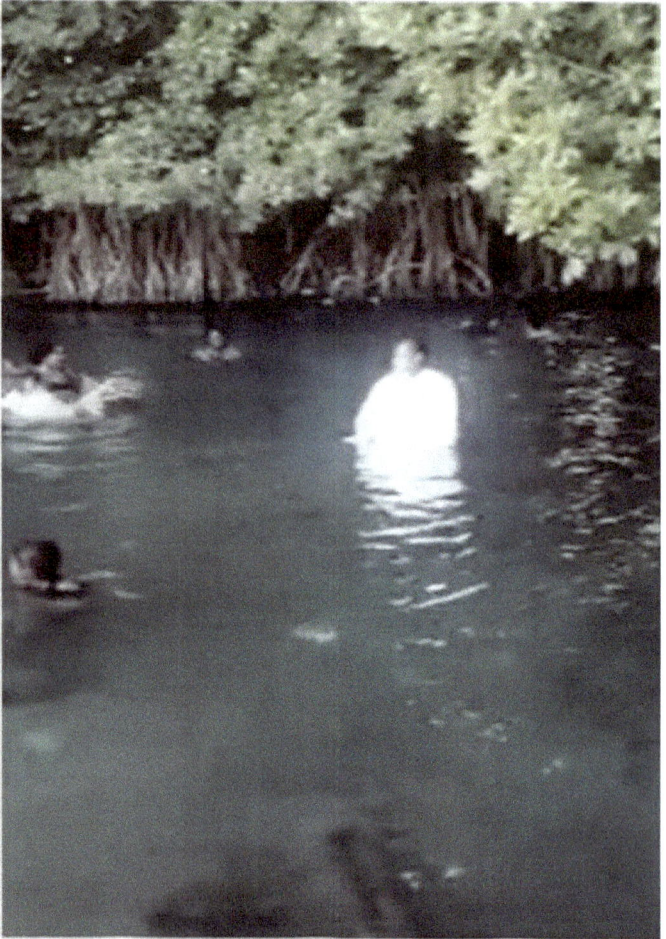

Fig. 2 The glory could be seen around me as I blessed the water.

The Angel of His Presence

Fig. 3 The Angel of His Presence appeared with us in the water March 21, 2021.

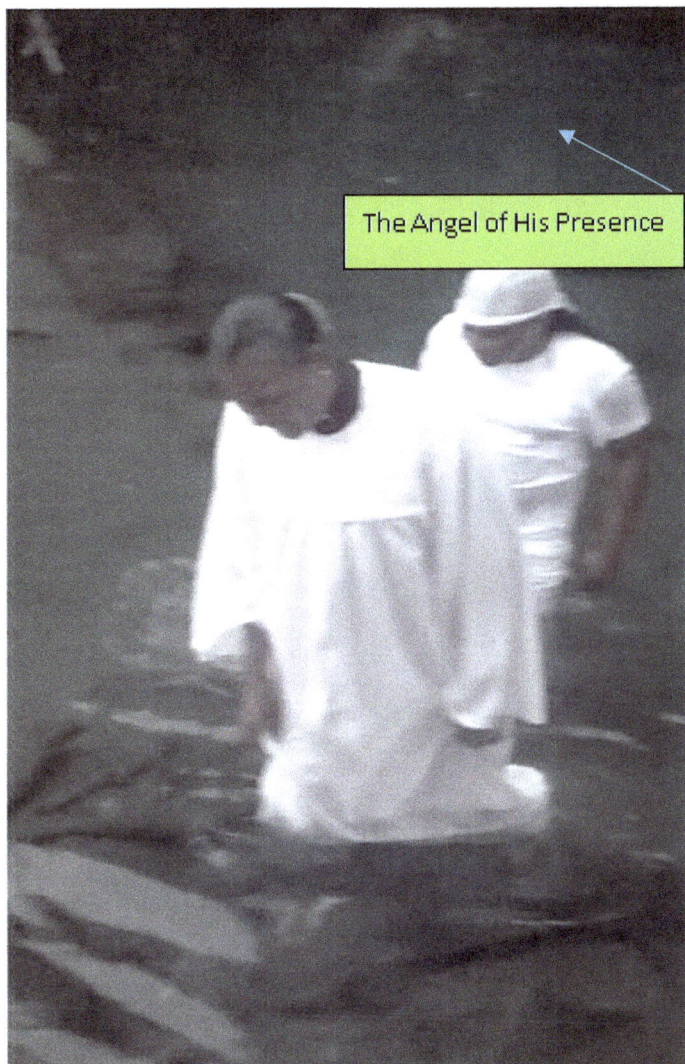

The Angel of His Presence

Fig. 4 The Angel of His Presence came up over us as we came up out of the water March 21, 2021.

The Lord instructed that His church should pray for the glory using Scriptures which speaks of His glory. All scriptures given to me by the Lord to pray for the glory of God were taken from the New King James Version.

I invite you to pray with me....

WHAT IS THE GLORY OF GOD?

The Most High, Jehovah God, is the most glorious entity there is. His glory is His essence and His essence is LOVE, for God is love (1 John 4:16). God spoke of His glory several times throughout scriptures. Yet, one may ask: What is the glory of God? For us to discover God's glory, we must go where He reveals Himself. His glory was first displayed to the patriarchs of the Old Testament. The Hebrew word for glory is כָּבוֹד or kavod or its English pronunciation kabod, כָּבוֹד means weight and heaviness. If I may try to explain this in Jamaican terms, Jamaicans have a way of describing a man's worth or importance by saying "di man heavy like lead!"

In attempting to describe the full weight and heaviness of God, the psalmist wrote: The heavens declare the glory of God; and the firmament sheweth his handywork. Day unto day uttereth speech, and night unto night sheweth knowledge (Ps. 19:1). By this we understand that the heavens and all that is within it declares the glory of God. The majestic splendor of HIS being, is demonstrated in the universe. Science confirms that there are many galaxies, many planets and many stars, all of which are breathed out of His mouth (Ps. 33:6), each star named by Him (Ps. 147:4) and He tracks its course (Isa. 40:26) even before man knew the name of one star. He made them all by His glory and they bow down and worship Him (Neh. 9:6). How majestic and glorious is that? By HIS glory he takes one part of Hydrogen and two parts of Oxygen (gases) and makes Water (liquid). His glory created the first particle in an atom. The mysteries of God and what is, remains indescribable to man. He is present, past and future. He can go to hell and back as He pleases

(1Pet. 3:19-20) - the most damning and terrifying place that exist, whether in thought, experience or place. Jesus Christ of Nazareth was the only person who by His glory commanded the gates between life and death to be lifted so that the King of Glory shall come in (Ps. 24:7-10) and took back the keys of the curse of death and hell. The Ancient gates had to respond to the King of Glory. At the fall of Adam the earth was cursed. The glory displayed at Jesus' death broke the curse of death upon man and the earth so that the earth could no longer hold the bodies of the saints (Matt. 27:52-54). He created hell and is in control of hell and the devil himself (Matt. 25:41, Matt. 4:7). Hell He created to display the power of His glory (Col. 1:16) for He alone has power to cast into Hell (Luke 12:5).

Nothing exists outside of the glory of God! His glory is personified in His Son, where God became flesh and dwelt among us (John. 1:14) - all who believe in the testimony of Jesus Christ His Son, the King of Glory. Here we see that while He dwelt among us, He exists beyond the universe outside of time, and He comes and lives in us by His indwelling Holy Spirit (1Cor. 3:16; 6:19 and 2Cor. 6:16). He is in the material and the immaterial. He exists before anything else was. He is so much more than we could ever imagine. Anything that you desire Him to be, in His Son He is. There is no one word that can adequately describe Him. Hence, the many names of God, some of which are: Jehovah, YHWH, Jehovah Rapha, Jehovah Nissi, Elohim, Aba, El Olam, El Shaddai, Tzevaot, I AM THAT I AM, Ancient of Days, El Elyon, Adonai, King of Glory (and so many others). His names describe aspects of His nature, character and being. He is behind every atom and particle of what is natural, to include what is unnatural, seen or unseen, visible or invisible to the naked eyes, the only wise God whose power is omnipotent. Consider that God's angels are fiery beings (Rev 10:1-4) that guards and protects His glory, yet God needs no protection; remember his wrath is as dreadful as liquid fire (Isa. 66:15, Nahum 1:6, Ps. 97:3), yet His love is as tender as a dove.

The glory of God, His essence, which is love, was demonstrated at Calvary in that, God graciously gave us His Son (Rom. 8:32). For God so loved the world that He gave his only begotten Son, that whosoever believeth in Him, should not die but have everlasting life (John 3:16). His Love, He gave in glory to the world - His one and only Son, the King of Glory. O LORD, our Lord, how majestic is Your name in all the earth (Ps. 8:1)!

Man and the Glory of God

God at creation gave man His glory by creating man in His image and in his likeness. He gave man dominion over the fish of the sea, birds of the air and over every living thing that moved upon the earth (Gen. 1:26-28). But, man lost God's glory at the fall, (Gen 3:7). When the glory departed, man for the first time felt shame, nakedness, fear, exposure and unworthiness. God being LOVE, had to cover man with fig leaves, for love covers a multitude of sin (1 Pet. 4:8). Unrecognized to us today, we continue in this fig of love symbolically, as most piece of clothing is made from the fiber of plants desiring to cover our shame. But thanks be to God! Who restored man to his rightful place of glory at the cross through Jesus Christ His Son. He endured the cross in nakedness and shame so that once again we are clothed in His glory.

In this pursuit to invoke the glory, the Lord enlightened the eyes of my understanding so that I was able to see that everything from Genesis to Revelations is about the glory of God accessible to man through Jesus Christ of Nazareth, His Son, the King of Glory!

Jesus as the Glory Throughout the Old Testament.

This book may not be able to capture all that He has revealed. For like the Apostle John, I have come to understand that if everything was to have been written, there would not be enough books to hold the revelations of the glory. However, to give you a general glimpse into His glory, you will find it displayed in His Son.

He appeared as and displayed his glory in the rainbow after the flood, (Gen. 9:8-17).

He was the pillar of cloud by day and a pillar of fire by night over Israel (Ex.13:21-22, 14:19-31).

He was the fire burning in the bush that was not consumed (Ex. 3:1-17).

The glory of God is seen throughout scripture in every sign, wonder and miracle. Some examples displayed include:

*   At the Red Sea and the crossing of the River Jordan (Ex. 14:21-22, Josh. 3:15-17).
*   Over Mount Sinai (Ex. 24:16).
*   In Solomon's Temple (2 Chron. 7:1-3).
*   Over the tent of meeting (Ex. 40:34-38)
*   Upon Aaron's rod that budded, blossomed and bore fruit in one night (Num. 17:1-13)
*   As the manna from heaven (Ex. 16)
*   Water from the rock Ex. (Num. 20)
*   The bronze fiery serpent that brought healing (Num. 21:8-9)

* Sound of marching in the tree tops (2 Sam 5: 23-25)

* The fourth man in the fire (Dan. 3:19-27).

* As the Commander of the army of the LORD (Josh. 5:14)

Jesus as the Glory Throughout the New Testament.

The splendor of the glory continued throughout the New Testament. Examples include the glory displayed:

* At all of Jesus' miracles throughout the synoptic gospels Matthew, Mark, Luke, and John.

* Appearing around an angel of the Lord who announced the birth of the 'good news', Jesus Christ of Nazareth, (Luke 2:8-10).

* At the Mount of Transfiguration in the spirit of the prophets and to His Inner Circle, (Matt. 17:1-9)

* As the light that appeared and spoke to Saul on the road to Damascus, (Acts 9:1-7)

It is important to note that when His glory is manifested, it is displayed in power that produces positive change!

Albeit, it is evidenced throughout scripture, both under the old and the new covenant, that Jesus desires to and has given his glory to all believers (John 17: 20-26). The glory was prophesied to the true church, who shall display His glory, in Jesus' mighty name! In Haggai 2:9 the prophet proclaimed 'The latter glory of this house will be greater than the former,' says the Lord of hosts, 'and in this place I will give peace,' declares the Lord of hosts." Isaiah 60:1 prophesied, "Arise, shine; for your light has come, and the glory of the Lord has risen upon you. In Ephesians 3:21 Paul wrote to Him be the glory in the church and in Christ Jesus to all generations forever and ever. Amen. And in 2 Corinthians 3:18 He preached, But we all, with unveiled faces, beholding as in a mirror the glory of the Lord, are being transformed into the same image from glory to glory, just as from the Lord, the Spirit.

Men Who Asked for, Saw and Witnessed the Glory

Moses asked for the glory (Ex. 33:18-23), Daniel and Ezekiel saw the glory (Dan. 7: 9-14) (Ez. 1), Peter, James and John witnessed the glory (Matt. 17:1-13).

Benefits of the glory that mortal men have received, include but is not limited, because God is omniscient:

* Wisdom and Spiritual insights

* Revelations

* Signs, wonders and miracles

* Salvation

* The spirit of the prophets and prophecies

* Health and healing

* Divine shield and protection

Additionally, the glory is promised at His coming (Matt 24:30-31), His brightness shall slay the wicked (2 Thess. 2:8), and at the end of the age; It is the light of the city (Rev. 21:23; 22:5).

Now, since the glory of the Lord has been freely given to those who ran before us, how do we today as the *eleventh or last hour workers*, invoke the glory? Ask and it shall be given, seek and you shall find, knock and the door shall be opened unto you (Matt. 7:7). You invoke the glory by praying for the glory. However, when you have received the glory, it is important that you also guard the glory.

How to Guard the Glory?

God intends for man to carry His glory and so He gave His glory to mankind through His Son, the Lord Jesus Christ of Nazareth. When we sin we lose the glory. Romans 3:23 says "For all have sinned, and come short of the glory of God". Here we see that sin (the works of the Devil), removes the glory of God from our lives. But thanks be to God, who gave us Jesus to destroy the works of the devil! He who has Jesus doesn't continue in sin and so guards the glory, (see 1 John 3:5-10).

Repentance (acknowledging and turning from one's sin) also guards the glory of the Lord, brings His presence and that of the Holy Spirit with His fruit of glory. Acts 3:19 "Therefore repent and return, so that your sins may be wiped away, in order that times of refreshing may come from the presence of the Lord". The presence of the Lord over Israel represents the glory, a pillar of cloud by day and a pillar of fire by night. In Acts 2: 38

"Peter said to them, Repent each of you and be baptized in the name of Jesus Christ for the forgiveness of your sins; and you will receive the gift of the Holy Spirit.

As you guard the glory through daily repentance (daily turning away from sin) and loving your brother, the presence of the Lord and His Holy Spirit will become a constant shield around you.

Therefore, guard the glory with:

* Daily repentance
* Endeavouring to keep the unity of the Spirit in the bond of peace (Eph. 4:3).
* Fulfil the law of Christ by loving one another; as Christ have loved us, that is to forgive quickly, have mercy and bear one another's burdens, and so fulfil the law of Christ.
* And, by praying these two prayers every day:

41

Firstly,

My Father, my Father, your words are true, by them your servant is warned; in keeping them, there is great reward. But who can discern their own errors? Forgive my hidden faults. Keep your servant also from wilful sins; may they not rule over me. Then I will be blameless, innocent of great transgression. May these words of my mouth and this meditation of my heart be pleasing in your sight, LORD, my Rock and my Redeemer. Lord Jesus help me every day to guard your glory that you have given to me. Thank you in Jesus' name, amen.

Secondly,

God my Father, my Father, in the name of Jesus Christ of Nazareth help us at Holy Living Christian Ministries (insert the name of your ministry) to always endeavour to keep the unity of the Spirit in the bond of peace.

Father make us all as thou Father art in the Son and the Son in thee. Make also, that we may be one in You that the world may believe that thou hast sent the Son. Guard the glory which thou gives to the Son, which He has given to us, that we may be one, even as You and the Son are one: Christ in us, and thou in Him, that we may be made perfect in one; that the world may know that thou hast sent Your Son, and hast loved us, as thou hast loved Him.

Father, make us one by the will of Christ so that we also, whom thou hast given Him will be with Him where He is. May we behold His glory, which thou hast given Him: for thou love Him before the foundation of the world. Love us God and guard our unity from the wiles of the devil!

Lord Jesus, bind us together with cords that cannot be broken. Your three strand cord cannot be broken, love of the Father, the Son and the

Holy Spirit. Lord, let us at Holy Living Christian Ministries (insert the name of your ministry) love one another as you have loved us.

Let nothing be done through strife or vainglory; but in lowliness of mind let each esteem other better than themselves. Oh, Holy Father, I pray to You through Your Son the Lord Jesus Christ of Nazareth my Saviour. Hear me Father and have mercy. Guard our unity in Jesus' name I pray amen.

A General Prayer for the Glory of the Lord

Father and God of our Lord and Saviour, the Lord Jesus Christ, God of Glory, God of the Kabod, I come to you asking for Your kabod, in the name of Yashua, in the name of Jesus Christ of Nazareth, the Messiah the Anointed One of Glory. God of the Kabod, God of Glory, let Your glory fall upon me, Let Your glory fall upon Your Church (insert the name of your ministry). Let Your Glory Lord fall upon the people of God. Soak us in Your glory Lord, the glory of Your Father.

God my Father, my Father, give us Your glory. Soak my body in your glory. Soak my spirit in your glory. Soak my soul in your glory, soak my mind in your glory, soak my strength in your glory! God my father, soak your church, your people Lord God in Your glory. Let your church become untouchable to the evil of our age and of

45

our time. God my Father, soak us in Your glory. Soak us in the fire of Your glory, in the full weight and heaviness of Your glory Lord, yes Lord, soak us in the full weight and heaviness of Your Kabod.

God my Father soak our liver in Your kabod, soak our kabod, our liver, in Your kabod and let us live Lord. Father in the name of Jesus Christ of Nazareth, Your Son, our Saviour give us Your kabod. Soak all of our internal body organs in your kabod. Soak our:

* Respiratory system in your kabod,
* Cardiovascular system in your kabod,
* Reproductive system in your kabod,
* Digestive system in your kabod,
* Excretory/Urinary system in your kabod,
* Endocrine system in your kabod,
* Lymphatic system in your kabod,
* Nervous system in your kabod,

* Skeleton system in your kabod,

* Muscular system in your kabod,

* Integumentary system in your kabod,

Lord Jesus, soak our will Lord in Your kabod, yes Lord and let us live! Let us live in Your kabod, let us live Lord Jesus in and by Your kabod.

INVOKING THE GLORY OF THE LORD FROM THE CANONIZED SCRIPTURES

Praying for the Glory From the Book of Exodus

For it is written:

1. Exodus 3:2

READ ALOUD: And the Angel of the Lord appeared to him in a flame of fire from the midst of a bush. So he looked, and behold, the bush was burning with fire, but the bush was not consumed.

PRAY: Angel of the Lord, come and appear to us in a flame of fire as You did to Your servant Moses, come and soak us in Your glory so that we are not consumed, by the lies, deception and the things of this world. Lord we desire Your glory, give us Your glory.

48

2. Exodus 15:11

READ ALOUD: Who is like You, O Lord, among the gods? Who is like You, glorious in holiness, fearful in praises, doing wonders?

PRAY: Lord Jesus, do wonders in us O Lord. Soak Your church in Your glorious holiness. Soak us in Your fearful praise. Do wonders in us and soak us in Your glory.

3. Exodus 24:15-16

READ ALOUD: Then Moses went up into the mountain, and a cloud covered the mountain. Now the glory of the Lord rested on Mount Sinai, and the cloud covered it six days. And on the seventh day He called to Moses out of the midst of the cloud.

PRAY: Lord Jesus, let the glory of the Lord come and cover us as it covered the mountain. Let the glory of the Lord rest upon Your church as it rested on Mount Sinai. May you call to us out of the midst of Your glory and let our ears be attentive to answer Your call.

4. Exodus 33: 9-10

READ ALOUD: And it came to pass, when Moses entered the tabernacle that the pillar of cloud descended and stood at the door of the tabernacle, and the Lord talked with Moses. All the people saw the pillar of cloud standing at the tabernacle door, and all the people rose and worshiped, each man in his tent door.

PRAY: God my Father let Your glory, the pillar of cloud descend and stand at the door of our tabernacle, the tabernacle of our bodies, the tabernacle of our church and talk with me Lord, talk with us Lord Jesus. Let all the people see Your glory standing with us Your church, as You stood with Moses and let them rise up and worship You.

5. Exodus 33:18-19

READ ALOUD: And he said, "Please, show me Your glory." Then He said, "I will make all My goodness pass before you, and I will proclaim the name of the Lord before you."

PRAY: Lord please show us Your glory, please make all Your goodness pass before us and proclaim Your name, the name of the Lord before us. Do it in us Lord Jesus, show us Your glory.

6. Exodus 34:5-7

READ ALOUD: Now the Lord descended in the cloud and stood with him there, and proclaimed the name of the Lord. And the Lord passed before him and proclaimed, "The Lord, the Lord God, merciful and gracious, longsuffering, and abounding in goodness and truth, keeping mercy for thousands, forgiving iniquity and transgression and sin, by no means clearing the guilty, visiting the iniquity of the fathers upon the children and the children's children to the third and the fourth generation."

PRAY: Lord Jesus, proclaim your name among us. Let Your glory pass before us and proclaim Your name Lord God. O Lord proclaim Your name and Your mercies, Your graciousness, Your long suffering, Your goodness and truth among us. Keeping Your mercies towards us O God. Forgiving us of our iniquities, our transgressions and our sins, keeping us from guilt, because we believe and accept Your truth, the truth of Your Son, the Lord Jesus Christ of Nazareth. O Father protect the generation of those who believe. Hallelujah!

7. Exodus 40:34-35

READ ALOUD: Then the cloud covered the tabernacle of meeting, and the glory of the Lord filled the tabernacle. And Moses was not able to enter the tabernacle of meeting, because the cloud rested above it, and the glory of the Lord filled the tabernacle.

PRAY: Father God let Your glory, Your kabod, cover the tabernacle of our souls, our spirits, our minds, our bodies, and our strength so that nothing of this world and of the forces of darkness will be able to enter us to destroy us, because of Your glory O God that protects us. Let Your kabod rest in, above and around us. Lord Jesus, let Your glory, the glory of the Lord fill us.

Praying for the Glory From the Book of Numbers

It is written:

1. Numbers 14:21

READ ALOUD: But truly, as I live, all the earth shall be filled with the glory of the Lord.

PRAY: Mighty God, You have promised that, truly as You live, all the earth shall be filled with Your glory, honour Your word, Lord and fill us with Your glory. Lord Jesus fill us with Your glory. We seek Your glory, the glory of the Father, the one true and living God. Thank You Jesus.

Praying for the Glory From the Book of Deuteronomy

It is written:

1. Deuteronomy 5:24

READ ALOUD: And you said: "Surely the LORD our God has shown us His glory and His greatness, and we have heard His voice from the midst of the fire."

PRAY: Show us Your glory Lord our God and Your greatness, that we may hear Your voice from the midst of the fire of Your glory.

2. Deuteronomy 28:58

READ ALOUD: If you do not carefully observe all the words of this law that are written in this book, that you may fear this glorious and awesome name, THE LORD YOUR GOD.

PRAY: Lord soak us in Your glory that we may observe all Your words that are written in Your book, that we may fear Your glorious and awesome name, THE LORD OUR GOD!

Praying for the Glory From the Book of Judges

It is written:

1. Judges 13:20

READ ALOUD: It happened as the flame went up toward heaven from the altar—the Angel of the Lord ascended in the flame of the altar! When Manoah and his wife saw this, they fell on their faces to the ground.

PRAY: Lord our God, let the flame of Your glory go up from our prayers, let it go up from our bodies, from the altar of our bodies and our worship. Angel of the Lord ascend in the flame of Your glory and let men and women, husbands and wives and children worship You. God, You came down in the days of old. O Ancient of Days, come down and let Your glory fill us and let us worship You forever.

Praying for the Glory From the Book of 1 Kings

It is written:

1. 1 Kings 8:10-11

READ ALOUD: And it came to pass, when the priests came out of the holy place that the cloud filled the house of the Lord, so that the priests could not continue ministering because of the cloud; for the glory of the Lord filled the house of the Lord.

PRAY: Father let it come to pass, that the glory cloud of the Lord, come and fill our church, the house of the Lord.

Praying for the Glory From the Book of 1 Chronicles

It is written:

1. 1 Chronicles 29:11

READ ALOUD: Yours, O Lord, is the greatness, the power and the glory, the victory and the majesty; for all that is in heaven and in earth is Yours; Yours is the kingdom, O Lord, and You are exalted as head over all.

PRAY: O Lord, give us Your greatness Lord. Give us Your power. Give us Your victory. Give us Your glory Lord, so that we will not be consumed by this world.

2. 1 Chronicles 29:13

READ ALOUD: Now therefore, our God, we thank You, and praise Your glorious name.

PRAY: Now God our Father, we Your church thank You and praise Your glorious name.

3. 2 Chronicles 7:1-3

READ ALOUD: When Solomon had finished praying, fire came down from heaven and consumed the burnt offering and the sacrifices; and the glory of the Lord filled the temple. And the priests could not enter the house of the Lord, because the glory of the Lord had filled the Lord's house. When all the children of Israel saw how the fire came down, and the glory of the Lord on the temple, they bowed their faces to the ground on the pavement, and worshiped and praised the Lord….

PRAY: Father let Your people pray until fire come down and consume our praise and worship, our offering and our sacrifices, for a broken spirit and a contrite heart Lord You will not despise. Let Your glory Lord fill our church, our bodies, our souls, our minds and our strengths, that the people may see and bow down and worship You.

Praying for the Glory From the Book of Nehemiah

It is written:

1. Nehemiah 9:5

READ ALOUD: …Stand up and bless the Lord your God forever and ever! Blessed be Your glorious name, which is exalted above all blessing and praise!

PRAY: Heavenly Father we stand up and bless the Lord our God forever and ever. Blessed be

Your glorious name, which is exalted above all blessings and praise!

Praying for the Glory From the Book of Psalm

It is written:

1. Psalm 8:1

READ ALOUD: O Lord, our Lord, how excellent is Your name in all the earth, who have set Your glory above the heavens!

PRAY: O Lord our Lord how excellent is Your name in all the earth, set Your glory, set Your kabod above us and above our church Holy Living Christian Ministries (insert the name of your ministry). Lord Jesus, set Your kabod over us in the earth.

2. Psalm 19:1

READ ALOUD: The heavens declare the glory of God; and the firmament shows His handiwork.

PRAY: Lord Jesus let us declare Your glory, let us, Your church show Your handiwork.

3. Psalm 24:7-10

READ ALOUD: Lift up your heads, O ye gates; And be lifted up, ye everlasting doors; and the King of glory shall come in. Who is this King of glory? The Lord strong and mighty, the Lord mighty in battle. Lift up your heads, O ye gates; even lift them up, ye everlasting doors; and the King of glory shall come in. Who is this King of glory? The LORD of hosts, he is the King of glory. Selah.

PRAY: King of Glory, lift up the heads of our gates! Lift up the everlasting doors of our lives and come in. Be our God! Lord Jesus, be our King of Glory. Lord, You are strong and mighty. Fight for us, Your church in this year and beyond. You are mighty in battle. Let Your kabod fight for us, O Lord. Be our King of Glory. You are the Lord of Host, Jehovah Sabaoth our King of Glory.

4. Psalm 29:3

READ ALOUD: The voice of the Lord is over the waters; the God of Glory thunders; the Lord is over many waters.

PRAY: O voice of the Lord, be over our waters. God of Kabod, God of Glory thunder over us and protect us. You are over many waters. Lord be over our waters, protect our waters and our food in this year and beyond. O God of Glory protect our waters, our seas, our shores, our watersheds, our rivers and our springs and our wells. Protect our harbors and let us live.

5. Psalm 57:5

READ ALOUD: Be exalted, O God, above the heavens; let Your glory be above all the earth.

PRAY: Be exalted in our lives O Lord in this year and beyond. Let Your kabod, Your glory be above our church, above our lives, above our families, our relatives, our children, our husbands and our wives. Lord Jesus, let Your kabod be over our jobs. Lord Jesus preserve the jobs of all those who trust in Your holy glory.

6. Psalm 63:2

READ ALOUD: So I have looked for You in the sanctuary, to see Your power and Your glory.

PRAY: We have looked for You in our sanctuary to see Your power and Your glory. Jesus, let us see Your power. Let us see Your glory.

7. Psalm 72:19

READ ALOUD: Blessed be His glorious name forever! And let the whole earth be filled with His glory. Amen and Amen.

PRAY: Lord blessed be Your glorious name forever! Father let our whole lives, churches, cities, countries and communities be filled with Your glory. Amen and Amen.

8. Psalm 79:9

READ ALOUD/PRAY: Help us, O God of our salvation, for the glory of Your name; and deliver us, and provide atonement for our sins, for Your names' sake!

9. Psalm 93:1

READ ALOUD: The Lord reigns, He is clothed with majesty; the Lord is clothed, He has girded

Himself with strength; surely the world is established, so that it cannot be moved.

PRAY: Lord reign in our lives and in our church. Clothe us with Your majesty and gird us with your strength in this year and beyond. Let us stand in your glory against any 5G, 6G, 7G and every other g's of this world. By Your glory Lord, Your glory, Your kabod, O God let us stand. For surely the world is established by You and Your glory so that it cannot be moved. Let us, Your church not be moved by anything other than Your glory, the glory of the One true and living God!

10. Psalm 102:16

READ ALOUD: The Lord shall build up Zion; He shall appear in His glory.

PRAY: Lord, You have promised to build up Zion. Therefore, appear now in Your Glory and build up Your church. Lord Jesus, keep us from falling. Restore us to a glorious church, one that You can present to Yourself as a radiant church, holy, without stain or wrinkle, free from blemish and blameless. That You may intern present us faultless before the throne of Your Holy Father.

11. Psalm 104:1

READ ALOUD /PRAY: Bless the Lord, O my soul! O Lord my God, You are very great: You are clothed with honor and majesty.

12. Psalm 104:31

READ ALOUD: May the glory of the Lord endure forever; may the Lord rejoice in His works.

PRAY: May Your glory, Your Kabod, the Glory of the Lord endure forever. May You rejoice over Your church. May You rejoice over and in us O God, for we too are a part of Your works.

13. Psalm 111:3

READ ALOUD: His work is honourable and glorious, and His righteousness endures forever.

PRAY: Make us honourable Lord, make Your church glorious again. Cause Your righteousness to endure in us forever.

14. Psalm 113:4

READ ALOUD: The Lord is high above all nations, His glory above the heavens.

PRAY: Be high above our nation Lord. Be high above our church. Let Your glory above the heavens rest upon our nation. Rest Lord upon our church.

15. Psalm 138:5

READ ALOUD: Yes, they shall sing of the ways of the Lord, for great is the glory of the Lord.

PRAY: Yes, we Your church shall sing of Your ways, for great is the glory of the Lord.

16. Psalm 145:5

READ ALOUD: I will meditate on the glorious splendor of Your majesty, and on Your wondrous works.

PRAY: We, as a church shall meditate on the glorious splendor of Your majesty. We shall meditate on Your wondrous works.

17. Psalm 145:11-12

READ ALOUD: They shall speak of the glory of Your kingdom, and talk of Your power, to make known to the sons of men His mighty acts, and the glorious majesty of His kingdom.

PRAY: We shall speak of the glory of Your kingdom, and talk of Your power, to make known to the sons of men Your mighty acts, and the glorious majesty of Your kingdom.

Praying for the Glory From the Book of Isaiah

It is written:

1. Isaiah 4:5

READ ALOUD: Then the Lord will create above every dwelling place of Mount Zion, and above her assemblies, a cloud and smoke by day and the shining of a flaming fire by night. For over all the glory there will be a covering.

PRAY: Lord Jesus, God of the Kabod, King of Glory, create over every dwelling place of the people of Mount Zion, Your church, the body of Christ and above all her assemblies, a cloud and a smoke of Your kabod by day and the shining of a flaming fire of Your kabod by night. For over all the glory, there will be a covering over us in this year and beyond. Thank You Jesus. Thank You Lord of the Kabod. You are the King of Glory. We worship You for Your kabod. We praise You for the covering of Your glory.

2. Isaiah 6:3

READ ALOUD: And one cried to another and said, "Holy, Holy, Holy, is the Lord of hosts; the whole earth is full of His glory!"

PRAY: We will cry one to another and say, "Holy, Holy, Holy is the Lord of hosts, the whole earth is full of Your glory".

3. Isaiah 12:5 and Isaiah 35:2

READ ALOUD: Sing to the Lord, for He has done excellent things; this is known in all the earth.

READ ALOUD: It shall blossom abundantly and rejoice, even with joy and singing. The glory of

Lebanon shall be given to it, the excellence of Carmel and Sharon. They shall see the glory of the Lord, the Excellency of our God.

PRAY: Lord Jesus, King of Glory, Lord of the Kabod, let us sing to You Lord for You have done excellent things. We shall blossom abundantly and rejoice even with joy and singing. For the glory of Lebanon shall be given to me/us your church, the excellence of Carmel and Sharon and the people shall see the glory of the Lord and the Excellency of our God.

4. Isaiah 42:8

READ ALOUD: I am the Lord, that is My name; and My glory I will not give to another, nor My praise to carved images.

PRAY: God my Father, my Father, You are Lord. That is Your name! Your glory You will not give to another god, nor Your praise to carved images.

71

But, O God You will give Your glory to Your children. Father, I thank You that You give us, Your children all of Your kabod for only in Your kabod will we live.

5. Isaiah 49:3

READ ALOUD: And He said to me, "You are My servant, O Israel, in whom I will be glorified."

PRAY: Lord Jesus You said that I am Your servant, O God of Israel in whom I shall be glorified because of Your Son, glorify yourself in me.

6. Isaiah 59:19

READ ALOUD: So shall they fear the name of the Lord from the west, and His glory from the rising of the sun; when the enemy comes in, like a flood the Spirit of the Lord will lift up a standard against him.

PRAY: Lord Jesus, King of Glory, Lord of the Kabod, we shall fear Your name from the west and Your glory from the rising of the sun. When the enemy comes in like a flood, the Spirit of the Lord, the King of Glory will lift up a standard, the standard of Your glory, word and truth against him!

7.   Isaiah 60:1-2

READ ALOUD: Arise, shine; for your light has come! And the glory of the Lord is risen upon you. For behold, the darkness shall cover the earth, and deep darkness the people; but the Lord will arise over you, and His glory will be seen upon you.

PRAY: My Father, my Father, God of Glory arise and shine. Shine upon me for Your light has come. Let my light come. Let the glory of the Lord rise upon me and Your church. Let it rise. For even though darkness shall cover the earth and

73

deep darkness the people, the Lord will arise over me/us and His glory, His kabod will be seen upon me/us. Lord let Your kabod arise over Your church, Holy Living Christian Ministries (insert the name of your ministry), let Your glory rise over the entire Body of the Lord Jesus Christ, let Your glory rise upon this Your church and Your glory be seen upon us.

8. Isaiah 60:19-21

READ ALOUD: The sun shall no longer be your light by day, nor for brightness shall the moon give light to you; but the Lord will be to you an everlasting light, and your God your glory. Your sun shall no longer go down, nor shall your moon withdraw itself; for the Lord will be your everlasting light, and the days of your mourning shall be ended. Also your people shall all be righteous; they shall inherit the land forever, the branch of My planting, the work of My hands, that I may be glorified.

PRAY: Lord God of glory, be our everlasting light O God of Glory, be our everlasting light! O God be our glory in this year and beyond. Let not our sun go down, or our moon withdraws itself, for You O God, is our everlasting light. O God do not let us mourn in this year or beyond. Protect us from Covid 19 and all forms of sicknesses that it shall bring or that may otherwise come. God my Father, my Father, let our days of mourning come to an end. Let Your people be righteous and in right standing with You. Let us inherit the land of Your glory and goodness forever. You have promised that the meek shall inherit the earth and that those who mourn shall be comforted. God of the Kabod, King of Glory, let us Your church, Holy Living Christian Ministries, (insert the name of your ministry) be the branch of Your planting, the works of Your hands. May You be glorified in us and in our ministry, in Jesus mighty name!

9. Isaiah 62:3

READ ALOUD: You shall also be a crown of glory in the hand of the Lord, and a royal diadem in the hand of your God.

PRAY: Lord Jesus, let Your church be a crown of glory in Your hand Lord, let us become a royal diadem in Your hand God.

Praying for the Glory From the Book of Ezekiel

It is written:

1. Ezekiel 1:26-28

READ ALOUD: And above the firmament over their heads was the likeness of a throne, in appearance like a sapphire stone; on the likeness of the throne was a likeness with the appearance of a man high above it. Also from the appearance of His waist and upward I saw, as it were, the color of amber with the appearance of fire all around within it; and from the appearance of His waist and downward I saw, as it were, the appearance of fire with brightness all around. Like the appearance of a rainbow in a cloud on a rainy day, so was the appearance of the brightness all around it. This was the appearance of the likeness of the glory of the Lord.

PRAY: Lord of the Kabod, God of Glory, King of Glory, above the firmament over our heads, is the likeness of Your throne, like a sapphire stone on the likeness of Your throne, let the likeness of your appearance be upon us. Let the likeness of Your appearance be upon us Your church. Be lifted high above us Lord. Let the fire of Your glory from Your waist upward be upon us. Let the fire of Your glory from your waist down be all around us. Engulf us Lord in the fire of Your glory. O covenant keeping God of the Kabod, the God who gives the rainbow and keeps His covenant with the earth and all of mankind, keep Your covenant of eternal mercy through Your Son, the Lord Jesus Christ of Nazareth, our Saviour and soon coming King. Let the appearance of Your glory, be all around us. Save us Lord. Do not let us be condemned with this world. Do not destroy all life. Save us from the flood and wave of deception and lies of this Dark Age. Covenant keeping God of the Kabod, remember the covenant of Your glory O God of the Kabod. Keep us in the cloud and rainbow of Your glory, Your kabod. Keep us in the Arch Keshet of Your kabod.

2. Ezekiel 3:12

READ ALOUD: Then the spirit took me up, and I heard behind me a voice of a great rushing, saying, Blessed be the glory of the LORD from his place.

PRAY: LORD! God My Father, my Father let Your spirit take us up and let us in one voice pray, "Blessed be the glory of the LORD from His place. Let the hand of the LORD be strong upon us during this year and beyond; let us never cease to give Your glory praise."

3. Ezekiel 3:23-27

READ ALOUD: Then I arose, and went forth into the plain: and, behold, the glory of the LORD stood there, as the glory which I saw by the river of Chebar: and I fell on my face. Then the spirit entered into me, and set me upon my feet, and spake with me, and said unto me, Go, shut thyself within thine house. But thou, O son of man, behold, they shall put bands upon thee, and shall bind thee with them, and thou shalt not go out among them: And I will make thy tongue cleave to the roof of thy mouth, that thou shalt be dumb, and shalt not be to them a reprover: for they are a rebellious house. But when I speak with thee, I will open thy mouth, and thou shalt say unto them, Thus saith the Lord GOD; He that heareth, let him hear; and he that forbeareth, let him forbear: for they are a rebellious house.

PRAY: Lord Jesus, let us behold Your glory, the glory of the LORD. Let it stands over us Your church I pray. That same glory that your servant Ezekiel saw by the river of Chebar, cause us to behold Your glory and fall upon our faces and give You praise. God our Father, let Your Spirit speak to us in this hour and raise us upon our feet that we may go shut ourselves within our houses and pray. Let us be silent before thee in prayer, that we may hear what your Spirit says. Then you will open our mouths and we shall say: Thus saith the Lord GOD; "He that heareth, let him hear; and he that forbeareth, let him forbear: for they are a rebellious house".

4. Ezekiel 8:4

READ ALOUD: And behold, the glory of the God of Israel was there, like the vision that I saw in the plain.

PRAY: Glory of the God of Israel, come and be with us, come and be with us in this age, as You were with Ezekiel.

5. Ezekiel 9:3

READ ALOUD: Now the glory of the God of Israel had gone up from the cherub, where it had been, to the threshold of the temple. And He called to the man clothed with linen, who had the writer's inkhorn at his side.

PRAY: God of Glory, the glory of the God of Israel, come to the threshold of our temple, the temple of our bodies and of our soul, of our mind, of our spirit and of our strength. Glory of God, the God of Israel come to the threshold of our church. Come to the threshold of our temple with the man clothed in linen and write Your glory at our sides by Your Spirit Lord, Your Holy Spirit. The piercing of Your side Lord Jesus, from which water and blood gushed Lord to wash our sins away forever, for good! For there are three that bears witness in the earth, the spirt, and the water and the blood. These three agree in one. Let the piercing of Your side be an eternal glory that comes to the threshold of our temples, for our bodies are the temple of the living God. Make us holy, make us pure. God of glory, give us Your glory.

6. Ezekiel 10:4

READ ALOUD: Then the glory of the LORD went up from the cherub and stood over the threshold of the house; and the house was filled with the cloud, and the court was full of the brightness of the LORD'S glory.

PRAY: God my Father, my father, let your glory rise upon us. Let it stand over the threshold of our bodies, our minds, our souls, our spirits, our strengths, our houses and thy house. Let us, thy temple and thine sanctuaries be filled with the cloud of Your shekinah glory, and the courts be full of the brightness of the LORD'S glory.

7. Ezekiel 10:18

READ ALOUD: Then the glory of the LORD departed from off the threshold of the house and stood over the cherubims.

PRAY: Lord Jesus, let your glory stand over the cherubim assign to the churches, that they may guard the glory of your house in these last days unto thine imminent return.

8. Ezekiel 10:19

READ ALOUD: And the cherubim lifted their wings and mounted up from the earth in my sight. When they went out, the wheels were beside them; and they stood at the door of the east gate of the Lord's house, and the glory of the God of Israel was above them.

PRAY: God of Israel, let us be lifted up as the cherubim from the earth and let Your wheels be beside us. Let the cherubim assigned to Holy Living Christian Ministries (insert the name of your church) stand at the door of the east gate of our church. Let Your glory, the glory of the God of Israel be above them and above our church to protect, to guard, to encamp and help us to guard the glory, to guard the holiness and righteousness that have been entrusted to us.

9. Ezekiel 11:22-25

READ ALOUD: Then did the cherubims lift up their wings, and the wheels beside them; and the glory of the God of Israel was over them above. And the glory of the LORD went up from the midst of the city and stood upon the mountain which is on the east side of the city. Afterwards the spirit took me up and brought me in a vision by the Spirit of God into Chaldea, to them of the captivity. So, the vision that I had seen went up from me. Then I spake unto them of the captivity all the things that the LORD had shewed me.

PRAY: Lord Jesus, Let the glory of the God of Israel be over our cherubim and stand in the midst of our streets and our cities and every mountain in this nation. Let it give us visions so that we may warn the cities onto repentance and the righteousness of God; that all men may hear and tremble at the knowledge of thy Son and humbly accept thy gift of salvation. Let Your glory come now Lord and never depart from us.

10. Ezekiel 39:21-22

READ ALOUD: And I will set my glory among the heathen, and all the heathen shall see my judgment that I have executed, and my hand that I have laid upon them. So, the house of Israel shall know that I am the LORD their God from that day and forward.

PRAY: Lord Jesus, set you glory among the heathen that they may see Your judgment that You have executed, and your hand that You have laid upon them. Let Your church know that You are the LORD their God from this day and forward. By Your glory defend and protect Your church from the works of the heathen and the evil one. Lord Jesus Christ of Nazareth, King of Glory, defend and protect us by thy glory this year and beyond.

11. Ezekiel 43:1-5

READ ALOUD: Afterward he brought me to the gate, the gate that faces toward the east. And behold, the glory of the God of Israel came from the way of the east. His voice was like the sound of many waters; and the earth shone with His glory. It was like the appearance of the vision which I saw — like the vision which I saw when I came to destroy the city. The visions were like the vision which I saw by the River Chebar; and I fell on my face. And the glory of the Lord came into the temple by way of the gate which faces toward the east. The Spirit lifted me up and brought me into the inner court; and behold, the glory of the Lord filled the temple.

PRAY: Lord Jesus, God of the Kabod, God of the east gate, let Your glory, the glory of the God of Israel come from the way of the east upon us, Your church. Speak to us and let us shine with

87

Your glory. Let Your glory destroy the iniquity in the city of Banbury, Linstead Saint Catherine, Jamaica (input the name of the city/country/nation that you are praying for) and spread miles and miles to surrounding cites streets, lanes and neighborhoods and countries in Jesus' name. Let Banbury, Linstead Saint Catherine, Jamaica (input the name of the city/country/nation that you are praying for) and its surroundings fall on their faces and worship You. Come Lord of Glory, let the Lord of Glory come into our temple and our cities by way of the east gate. Lift us by Your Holy Spirit and bring me and this church into Your inner courts, the inner courts of Your glory. Let the glory of the Lord fill me and Your people. Fill our temples and Your sanctuary in Jesus mighty name.

12. Ezekiel 44:4

READ ALOUD: Then brought he me the way of the north gate before the house: and I looked, and behold, the glory of the LORD filled the house of the LORD: and I fell upon my face.

PRAY: Lord God my father, my Father, let us look and behold Your glory. Give us Your glory I pray. You are coming back for a glorious church, so Lord give us Your glory. Bring back the sanctity of the church, Your sanctuary, of thy temple and thy holy place. That we may again observe your ordinances, decrees and keep Your laws and statutes in all Your assemblies. We shall again hallow Your Sabbath days and offer You worship through grace in Jesus Christ Your Son. Amen!

Praying for the Glory From the Book of Habakkuk

It is written:

1. Habakkuk 2:14

READ ALOUD: For the earth will be filled with the knowledge of the glory of the Lord, as the waters cover the sea.

PRAY: God my Father, my Father, Aba Father, fill the earth with the knowledge of the glory of You just as the waters cover the sea. For the earth is the Lord's and the fullness there of and they that dwell therein. Lord Jesus, let Your glory fill Your church. Let Your glory fill the earth Lord this year and beyond. Empower Your true church, Son of the living God, who says upon this rock I build My church and the gates of hell shall not prevail against it. Therefore, by the power and the promise in Your word, let Your glory return to

Your Church Lord Jesus Christ of Nazareth. Father, let the earth be filled with the knowledge of Your Son! Let our church, Your people, be filled with the knowledge of the glory of the Lord Jesus Christ of Nazareth, as the waters cover the sea. Let everything that dwells in the earth know You Lord in this year and beyond.

2. Habakkuk 3:3

READ ALOUD: God came from Teman, the Holy One from Mount Paran. Selah. His glory covered the heavens, and the earth was full of His praise.

PRAY: God, You came from Teman. Holy One of Israel from Mount Paran, come to us from the south Lord. Dawn over us, shine forth from mount Paran. Let Your glory that covers the heavens shine forth upon us Your children. Let Your glory cloud come and rest upon us as it did in the desert of Paran. Come to us Lord with myriads of Your holy ones, from Your right hand.

91

Be a fiery law for us to protect us against Corona virus and all its variants. Protect Your church from all diseases and viruses launched on the earth by the god of this world and let the whole earth be full of Your praise.

3. Habakkuk 3:4

READ ALOUD: His brightness was like the light; He had rays flashing from His hand, and there His power was hidden.

PRAY: Lord God our Father, let Your brightness be our light and the rays flashing from Your hand, a sword that protect us. Let Your hidden power be our shield against all diseases, germs, viruses, known and unknown, seen or unseen, visible or invisible, spiritual or manmade. O God of the Kabod, give us Your glory and let Your glory protect us from the attacks of the enemy. For he who dwells in the secret place of the Most High, shall abide under the shadow of the Almighty.

You, who was wounded for our transgressions, bruised for our iniquities, on whom the chastisement that brought us peace was laid. It was laid upon You Lord and by Your stripes Lord we are healed.

Praying for the Glory From the Book of Matthew

It is written:

1. Matthew 6:13

READ ALOUD: For Yours is the kingdom and the power and the glory forever. Amen.

PRAY: Lord Jesus you are the King of Glory. Yours is the kingdom, the power and the glory forever. Therefore, Lord I ask You to forever give us Your glory, Your power and Your kingdom. Amen

2. Matthew 17:5

READ ALOUD: While he was still speaking, behold, a bright cloud overshadowed them; and suddenly a voice came out of the cloud, saying, "This is My Beloved Son, in whom I am well pleased. Hear Him!"

PRAY: Lord Jesus, while you are still speaking to me, to us, to Your church in this hour, let the brightness of Your glory overshadow us. Let the Father's voice speak to us from the cloud of Your glory, confirming Your glory, Your power and Your kingdom. For we are well pleased Lord to hear and obey You the Son of God. Lord we desire to know the Father through the Son. Hallelujah!

3. Matthew 24:30

READ ALOUD: Then the sign of the Son of Man will appear in heaven, and then all the tribes of the earth will mourn, and they will see the Son of Man coming on the clouds of heaven with power and great glory.

PRAY: God of the Kabod, send the sign of the Son of man in the heaven and let the tribes of the earth mourn. But, let Your church, Your called out and chosen ones see the Son of Man coming on the clouds of heaven with power and great glory. Deliver us Lord from the hour of trial that shall come upon this earth to test the saints.

Praying for the Glory From the Book of Mark

It is written:

1. Mark 9:7

READ ALOUD: And a cloud came and overshadowed them; and a voice came out of the cloud, saying, "This is My Beloved Son. Hear Him!"

PRAY: God my Father who art in heaven, let the cloud of Your holy glory overshadow us and let

KAREL DAWES

Your voice come out of the cloud of Your glory
and speak to us. In this hour of great trial and
deception, tell us about Your beloved Son. Father,
Let the truth of the gospel go forth and let us hear
and obey Him. For no man can come to the Son,
except the Father enables him.

Praying for the Glory From the Book of Luke

It is written:

1. Luke 2:9

READ ALOUD: And behold, an angel of the
Lord stood before them, and the glory of the Lord
shone around them, and they were greatly afraid.

PRAY: Angel of the Lord, stand before Your
church, Your people and let Your glory shine
around us. Let us greatly fear Your glorious name
and worship You forever. Let Your glory come

and protect us as it did the children of Israel, a pillar of cloud by day and a pillar of fire by night.

2. Luke 9:34

READ ALOUD: While he was saying this, a cloud came and overshadowed them; and they were fearful as they entered the cloud.

PRAY: Lord Jesus let the cloud of Your glory overshadow us and let us enter Your glory cloud in holy fear of Your matchless name.

3. Luke 21:27

READ ALOUD: Then they will see the Son of Man coming in a cloud with power and great glory.

PRAY: O Son of Man, come with Your power and Your great glory. Give us Your power and Your great glory to withstand the sicknesses, lies, deception and persecution of our time, in this hour and in this age. Lord Jesus give us Your glory, the glory of the Father.

Praying for the Glory From the Book of John

It is written:

1. John 1:14

READ ALOUD: And the Word became flesh and dwelt among us, and we beheld His glory, the glory as of the only begotten of the Father, full of grace and truth.

PRAY: Lord Jesus, You are the WORD. You became flesh and dwelled among us, and Your disciples beheld Your glory. The glory of the only begotten of the Father, full of grace and truth. Now Lord, greater things You have said, we shall do because You go to the Father. You promised to ask Him and whatever we ask You will do it for us so that the Son may bring glory to the Father, now Lord give us, Your children Your glory. Fill us with Your Kabod. Fill us with Your grace and with Your truth and let us behold Your glory in our time, in this age and the age to come.

2. John 11:40

READ ALOUD: Jesus said to her, "Did I not say to you that if you would believe you would see the glory of God?"

PRAY: You promised Lord that if we believe we will see Your glory. Lord we believe, now show us Your glory.

3. John 13:31-32

READ ALOUD: So, when he had gone out, Jesus said, "Now the Son of Man is glorified, and God is glorified in Him. If God is glorified in Him, God will also glorify Him in Himself, and glorify Him immediately.

PRAY: Therefore, God my Father, my Father, if I am dead and my life is hidden in You by Christ Jesus, will You not also glorify me immediately? Lord I pray, give me Your glory. Soak me in Your glory and let me guard Your glory. Soak me in the full weight and heaviness of Your kabod. Let Your glory come and protect Your called out chosen ones Lord. Let it protect my body, my soul, my mind, my spirit and my strength.

4. John 17:5

READ ALOUD: And now, O Father, glorify Me together with Yourself, with the glory which I had with You before the world was.

PRAY: Now O Father and the Lord Jesus Christ my Saviour, glorify me and Your church together with Yourself, with the glory which Jesus had before the world was. Lord Jesus, glorify Your church with the glory before sin was. Lord Jesus make us holy for You are holy. Lord, keep us pure and in right standing with You. Lord Jesus give us Your glory and let us come to You as a spotless bride to a spotless lamb that laid down His life for His people.

Praying for the Glory From the Book of Acts

It is written:

1. Acts 7:2

READ ALOUD: And he said, "Brethren and fathers, listen: The God of glory appeared to our father Abraham when he was in Mesopotamia, before he dwelt in Haran."

PRAY: Lord God of Glory, you appeared to our Father Abraham when he was in Mesopotamia, when he was still in sin and before he dwelt in Haran. You appeared to him before he came out of a pagan lifestyle. God, you appeared to him in

Your glory while he was yet in sin. Now Lord Jesus, give us your glory. Give Your rebellious church Your glory by delivering us from sin. God we are not deserving, but we pray for your mercies. Appear to us in Your holy glory, O God of Glory and restore the glory of Your church.

2. Acts 7:55

READ ALOUD: But he, being full of the Holy Spirit, gazed into heaven and saw the glory of God, and Jesus standing at the right hand of God.

PRAY: Lord, let me and Your church be filled with Your Holy Spirit. Let the Holy Spirit be ever present among us. Let us gaze into heaven and see Your glory. The glory of God and Jesus standing at the right hand of God. Lord Jesus stand and defend Your body, the Body of Christ from the spirit of death, of persecution and of murder. Lord Jesus, by Your Glory deliver us from the spirits of Jezebel, Molech, Pharoah,

Goliath, Haman, Herod and all other spirits that seek to kill us and our children. In this hour, Lord Jesus, send us the spirits of Moses and of Elijah, by Your glorious power and restore Your glorious church before the great and terrible day of our Lord.

Praying for the Glory From the Book of Romans

It is written:

1. Romans 8:17

READ ALOUD: And if children, then heirs— heirs of God and joint heirs with Christ, if indeed we suffer with Him, that we may also be glorified together.

PRAY: Lord Jesus, You said we are children, then heirs, heirs of God and joint heirs with Christ. If indeed we suffer with Him, then we will also be glorified together. Lord glorify us with the glory that You Yourself have received from God.

Praying for the Glory From the Book of Corinthians

It is written:

1. 2 Corinthians 3:18

READ ALOUD: But we all, with unveiled face, beholding as in a mirror the glory of the Lord, are being transformed into the same image from glory to glory, just as by the Spirit of the Lord.

PRAY: Lord Jesus unveil our faces and let us behold Your glory and be transformed into the same image of the glory of God from glory to glory just as by Your Spirit.

2. 2 Corinthians 4:6

READ ALOUD: For it is the God who commanded light to shine out of darkness, who has shone in our hearts to give the light of the knowledge of the glory of God in the face of Jesus Christ.

PRAY: Now Lord God, command light to shine out of us. Shine in our hearts and give us the light of the knowledge of the glory of God in the face of Jesus Christ.

Praying for the Glory From the Book of Ephesians

It is written:

1. Ephesians 3:21

READ ALOUD: To Him be glory in the church by Christ Jesus to all generations, forever and ever. Amen.

PRAY: To You Lord, be glory in the church by Christ Jesus to all generations, forever and ever. Amen.

Praying for the Glory From the Book of Colossians

It is written:

1. Colossians 1:27

READ ALOUD: To them God willed to make known what are the riches of the glory of this mystery among the Gentiles: which is Christ in you, the hope of glory.

PRAY: Father I ask, I seek, I knock on the door of Your glory. God it is Your will to make known the riches of Your glorious mystery in Christ – the great hope of glory. Lord make known to me/us Your glory in this year and beyond.

Praying for the Glory From the Book of 1 Thessalonians

It is written:

1. 1 Thessalonians 2:12

READ ALOUD: That you would walk worthy of God who calls you into His own kingdom and glory.

PRAY: God my Father, I pray that I may walk worthy of You, who have called me into Your own kingdom and glory. Thank You Jesus that you empower Your church to walk worthy of Your glory.

Praying for the Glory From the Book of Hebrews

It is written:

1. Hebrews 1:3

READ ALOUD: Who being the brightness of His glory and the express image of His person, and upholding all things by the word of His power, when He had by Himself purged our sins, sat down at the right hand of the Majesty on high.

PRAY: Lord Jesus, You purged me of my sins at Calvary, therefore let me live in the finished work of the cross. Let me sit down and rest in the right standing that You have prepared for me with the Majesty on High, who sits on the throne of His glory.

2. Hebrews 2:9

READ ALOUD: But we see Jesus, who was made a little lower than the angels, for the suffering of death crowned with glory and honor, that He, by the grace of God, might taste death for everyone.

PRAY: Lord Jesus, You were made a little lower than the angels that You may suffer death to be crowned with glory and honour. It was by Gods' grace that You tasted death for everyone so that we might live. Lord, I thank You that You give us Your glory, so that we may live! Now crown us and honour us Your church with Your glory, for You have paid the full price for our sins. Hallelujah! Thank You Jesus.

Praying for the Glory From the Book of 1 Peter

It is written:

1. 1 Peter 5:10

READ ALOUD: But may the God of all grace, who called us to His eternal glory by Christ Jesus, after you have suffered a while, perfect, establish, strengthen, and settle you.

PRAY: Lord Jesus, we have suffered a while, now shortened the days of our sufferings. God of all grace, who called us to His eternal glory by Christ Jesus, begin to perfect us. Establish us, strengthen us, and settle us in Your glory.

2. 2 Peter 1:17

READ ALOUD: For He received from God the Father honor and glory when such a voice came to Him from the Excellent Glory: "This is My Beloved Son, in whom I am well pleased."

PRAY: God whose name and voice is His Excellent glory. Give us Your honour and Your glory because of Your beloved son who live in us by the Spirit. Let us please You God because of the glory of the Son in whom You are well pleased.

Praying for the Glory From the Book of Revelation

It is written:

1. Revelation 15:8

READ ALOUD: The temple was filled with smoke from the glory of God and from His power....

PRAY: Therefore, O Lord, let our temples be filled with the smoke from Your glory O God and from Your power. Fill us Lord with Your Shekinah glory.

2. Revelation 19:1

READ ALOUD: After these things, I heard a loud voice of a great multitude in heaven, saying, "Alleluia! Salvation and glory and honor and power belong to the Lord our God!"

111

PRAY: So that after these things, we may be part of the loud voice of the great multitude in heaven, saying Alleluia! Salvation and glory and honor and power belong to the Lord our God!"

3. Revelation 21:23

READ ALOUD: The city had no need of the sun or of the moon to shine in it, for the glory of God illuminated it. The Lamb is its light.

PRAY: Lord God, my Father, my Father, let our bodies, our church, our cities and our nation shine with the glory of God. For we need no other light to illuminate us but Your Glory. Let the Lamb of God be our eternal light today and forever and ever. Amen!

INVOKING THE GLORY OF THE LORD FROM THE APOCRYPHA

Praying for the Glory From 1 Esdras

It is written:

1. 1 Esdras 4:59

READ ALOUD: From thee cometh victory, from thee cometh wisdom, and thine is the glory, and I am thy servant.

PRAY: God my Father, my Father, in the name of Jesus Christ of Nazareth, I thank You that from thee O God comes victory, from thee cometh wisdom and thine is the glory. I am thy servant O God, therefore give me the victory, give me thy wisdom, give me thy glory and help me to guard the glory given me.

2. 1 Esdras 5:61

READ ALOUD: And they sung with loud voices songs to the praise of the Lord, because his mercy and glory is forever in all Israel.

PRAY: God my Father, my Father, let me sing songs of praises to You Lord, because Your mercy and glory is forever and forever in all of Jamaica (input your country).

Praying for the Glory From 2 Esdras

It is written:

1. 2 Esdras 2:36

READ ALOUD: Flee the shadow of this world, receive the joyfulness of your glory: I testify my Saviour openly.

PRAY: God my Father, my Father, give me (us) the joyfulness of Your glory that we may flee the shadow of this world and openly testify of my (our) Saviour, the Lord Jesus Christ of Nazareth.

2. 2 Esdras 3:19

READ ALOUD: And thy glory went through four gates, of fire, and of earthquake, and of wind, and of cold; that thou mightest give the law unto the seed of Jacob, and diligence unto the generation of Israel.

PRAY: Let thy glory come through four gates, of fire, and of earthquake, and of wind, and of cold; and give us the seed of Jacob Your law and diligence unto the generation of Israel and to thy Church.

3. 2 Esdras 7:52

READ ALOUD: And that the glory of the most High is kept to defend them which have led a wary life, whereas we have walked in the most wicked ways of all?

115

PRAY: Lord, we have walked in the most wicked ways of all and we are undeserving. But, give us the glory of the Most High, Your glory which is kept to defend them which have led a wary life.

4. 2 Esdras 8:21

READ ALOUD: Whose throne is inestimable; whose glory may not be comprehended; before whom the hosts of angels stand with trembling,

PRAY: Father, Your, throne is immeasurable; Your glory unfathomable. Before You the hosts of angels stand with trembling.

5. 2 Esdras 8:30

READ ALOUD: Take thou no indignation at them which are deemed worse than beasts; but love them that always put their trust in thy righteousness and glory.

PRAY: Father, through Your Son Jesus Christ have mercy upon us. Take no indignation at them which are deemed worse than beasts; but love them that always put their trust in thy righteousness and in thine glory.

6. 2 Esdras 8:51

READ ALOUD: But understand thou for thyself, and seek out the glory for such as be like thee.

PRAY: So Father I seek out Your glory that I (we), Your church may be more like thee. Give us Your glory. Thank You Jesus!

7. 2 Esdras 16:12

READ ALOUD: The earth quaketh, and the foundations thereof; the sea ariseth up with waves from the deep, and the waves of it are troubled, and the fishes thereof also, before the Lord, and before the glory of his power:

PRAY: Father, the earth and the seas and the foundations and the contents thereof quake and are troubled before You, and before the glory of Your power. Therefore, I pray that You will give us Your glory. Give us Your power to stand in the midst of this great trial and tribulation. We firmly believe in Your power and glory that protect us.

8. 2 Esdras 16:53

READ ALOUD: Let not the sinner say that he hath not sinned: for God shall burn coals of fire upon his head, which saith before the Lord God and his glory, I have not sinned.

PRAY: Lord, we confess that we are sinners, saved only because of Your grace and great mercies which endureth forever. Before You Lord God, we pray for Your glory. Let it become a shield around us and the lifter up of our heads.

Praying for the Glory From Tobit

It is written:

1. Tobit 12:15

READ ALOUD: I am Raphael, one of the seven holy angels, which present the prayers of the saints, and which go in and out before the glory of the Holy One.

PRAY: Lord God Almighty, Jehovah Rapha is Your name. Send Arch Angel Raphael, one of Your holy angels which present the prayers of the saints and which go in and out before the glory of You, the Holy One. Send Raphael Lord as You sent him to Tobit thy faithful servant. Send him with the healing balm to Your people. Let him teach us the secret healing powers of the kingdom. Lord Jesus, send Raphael for he is a ministering angel of healing sent to serve the heirs of salvation. O Glory be to the true and living God and to Him alone!

Praying for the Glory From the Wisdom of Solomon

It is written:

1. Wisdom of Solomon 7:25

READ ALOUD: For she is the breath of the power of God, and a pure influence flowing from the glory of the Almighty: therefore, can no defiled thing fall into her.

PRAY: Lord God, give us Your church the wisdom of Your glory, the breath and power of God, Your pure influence flowing from the glory of the Almighty, so that we may not accept any defiled thing.

2. Wisdom of Solomon 9:10

READ ALOUD: O send her out of thy holy heavens, and from the throne of thy glory, that being present she may labour with me, that I may know what is pleasing unto thee.

PRAY: Lord from Your throne of glory send us Your wisdom, that we may know and do what pleases You and not be deceived by any power. Help us to keep steadfast in Your wisdom and glory. Let us by Your wisdom exercise faith in these times, that when You come, You may find faith in the earth.

Praying for the Glory From Sirach

It is written:

1. Sirach 17:13

READ ALOUD: Their eyes saw the majesty of his glory, and their ears heard his glorious voice.

PRAY: Lord let our eyes see the majesty of Your glory, and our ears hear Your glorious voice.

2. Sirach 36:14

READ ALOUD: Fill Sion with thine unspeakable oracles, and thy people with thy glory:

PRAY: Father, fill us Your church with Your unspeakable visions, and with Your glory that we may discern the times and the seasons.

3. Sirach 42:16

READ ALOUD: The sun that giveth light looketh upon all things, and the work thereof is full of the glory of the Lord.

PRAY: Father, just as the sun giveth light to look upon all things, give us Your glory. Let Your glory give us light to examine all things and to discern all works. Make us full of Your glory that we may not be deceived or blinded by the god of this world.

4. Sirach 42:17

READ ALOUD: The Lord hath not given power to the saints to declare all his marvellous works, which the Almighty Lord firmly settled, that whatsoever is, might be established for his glory.

PRAY: Lord Jesus, give us Your glory and establish Your people, Your saints, Your church for Your glory. Let everything that we do be for Your glory, for You are the head and the glory of the church.

Praying for the Glory From Baruch

It is written:

1. Baruch 4:24

READ ALOUD: Like as now the neighbours of Sion have seen your captivity: so shall they see shortly your salvation from our God which shall come upon you with great glory, and brightness of the Everlasting.

PRAY: Lord God Almighty, let Your salvation and brightness come upon Your church with great glory.

2. Baruch 4:37

READ ALOUD: Lo, thy sons come, whom thou sentest away, they come gathered together from the east to the west by the word of the Holy One, rejoicing in the glory of God.

PRAY: God my Father, let Your children come to You by the power of Your WORD, O Holy One of Israel and give us Your glory that we may rejoice in the glory of You.

3. Baruch 5:1

READ ALOUD: Put off, O Jerusalem, the garment of mourning and affliction, and put on the comeliness of the glory that cometh from God for ever.

PRAY: God of glory, give us Your glory. Let us put off the garment of mourning and affliction which began in 2019, this year and beyond. Today and forever, let us wear the beauty of the glory that comes from You Eternal God forever.

4. Baruch 5:2

READ ALOUD: Cast about thee a double garment of the righteousness which cometh from

God; and set a diadem on thine head of the glory of the Everlasting.

PRAY: Lord Jesus drape Your church with a double garment of the righteousness of God. Set a diadem of glory upon our heads, the glory of the Everlasting God forever.

5. Baruch 5:4

READ ALOUD: For thy name shall be called of God for ever The peace of righteousness, and The glory of God's worship.

PRAY: Lord, let us Your church be known by the glory of Your worship and by the peace of Your righteousness.

6. Baruch 5:6

READ ALOUD: For they departed from thee on foot, and were led away of their enemies: but God bringeth them unto thee exalted with glory, as children of the kingdom.

PRAY: Lord Jesus, as children of the kingdom, let us be exalted with Your glory. Lord God bring back the glory of Your church that nations may once again hope in You.

7. Baruch 5:7

READ ALOUD: For God hath appointed that every high hill, and banks of long continuance, should be cast down, and valleys filled up, to make even the ground that Israel may go safely in the glory of God

PRAY: Lord, lower every hill. Remove every persistent boundary and fill up the valleys so that we Your children may go safely into Your glory.

8. Baruch 5:9

READ ALOUD: For God shall lead Israel with joy in the light of his glory with the mercy and righteousness that cometh from him.

PRAY: Lord God, lead Your church with joy in the light of Your glory and with the mercy and righteousness that cometh from Your Son the Lord Jesus Christ of Nazareth.

Praying for the Glory From Additions to the Book of Esther

It is written:

1. Additions to Esther 13:14

READ ALOUD: But I did this, that I might not prefer the glory of man above the glory of God: neither will I worship any but thee, O God, neither will I do it in pride.

PRAY: Lord God, I (we) desire Your glory and not the glory of man. I (we) will with great humility worship You only and not man.

Praying for the Glory From Additions to the Book of Daniel

It is written:

1. Additions to Daniel 1:20

READ ALOUD: Deliver us also according to thy marvellous works, and give glory to thy name, O Lord: and let all them that do thy servants hurt be ashamed;

PRAY: Father, deliver Your church according to thy marvelous works. Let every deceptive spirit be ashamed and give glory to thy matchless name.

2. Additions to Daniel 1:31

READ ALOUD: Blessed art thou in the temple of thine holy glory: and to be praised and glorified above all forever.

PRAY: Lord, you are blessed in the temple of Your holy glory and You are to be praised and glorified above all forever.

Praying for the Glory From 2 Maccabees

It is written:

1. 2 Maccabees 2:8

READ ALOUD: Then shall the Lord shew them these things, and the glory of the Lord shall appear, and the cloud also, as it was shewed under Moses, and as when Solomon desired that the place might be honourably sanctified.

PRAY: Father, show us Your glory. Let Your glory cloud appear in our midst just as in the day of Moses and as in Solomon's temple, so let Your glory come and fill our church in this year and beyond. Thank You Jesus Christ of Nazareth. Amen.

N.B. All Apocrypha scriptures found at Art and the Bible © 2005 - 2021 artbible.info. Retrieved from https://www.artbible.info/concordance/g/454-3.html

ABOUT THE AUTHOR

Prophet Reverend Karel Dawes, is an end time bond slave of the Lord Jesus Christ, chosen by God and not by the agency of man, to prepare the Body of Christ for His return. She is Senior Pastor and founder of Holy Living Christian Ministries, Banbury Linstead, Saint Catherine, Jamaica. Karel has a passion for the kingdom of God, raising up souls and transforming lives. This warrior, battles the forces of darkness by spending hours in the presence of the Lord in prayers, fasting and worship. This daughter in whom the Lord delights, has been gifted with spiritual insight into the word of God, the prophetic after the order of Elijah. In her seventeen (17) years of ministry, the anointing that carries her, has raised the dead, healed the sick, cast out demons, tread upon serpents and scorpions, break and nullifies obeah, witchcraft and every dark magic, spells and curses in Jesus mighty name. She takes from God and gives to the people by the power of the Holy Spirit. This daughter of Zion has been visited by the Lord Jesus Christ on several occasions, has been taken up into heaven in a vision and has received several visions from the Lord. She holds a BSc. In International Relations & Management Studies and a Masters in Divinity with special emphasis in Leadership and Management. By profession she is a Senior Project Analyst, married with three (3) beautiful children.

*9 7 8 1 9 5 4 7 5 5 1 3 0 *